D0230586

OWLS

OWLS

MATT SEWELL

EBURY
PRESS

3 5 7 9 10 8 6 4

Ebury Press, an imprint of Ebury Publishing
20 Vauxhall Bridge Road,
London, SW1V 2SA

Ebury Press is part of the Penguin Random House group
of companies whose addresses can be found at
global.penguinrandomhouse.com

Text and illustrations © Matt Sewell 2014

Matt Sewell has asserted his right to be identified as the author of this
Work in accordance with the Copyright, Designs and Patents Act 1988

First published by Ebury Press in 2014
www.eburypublishing.co.uk

A CIP catalogue record for this book is available from the British Library

Project editor: Nicki Crossley
Edited by: Kate Moore and Jane Sturrock
Series design by Two Associates; this edition compiled by Tash Webber

ISBN 978 0 09 195999 9

Printed and bound in Italy by Printer Trento
Colour origination by Altaimage, London

Penguin Random House is committed to a sustainable future for
our business, our readers and our planet. This book is made from
Forest Stewardship Council® certified paper.

For my goldfinches, Jess, Romy and Mae

CONTENTS

FOREWORD

Matt's latest book looks at our favourite
nocturnal, nonchalant birds of prey: the
Owl. Wide eyed in the still of night. Silent in
flight. A strange rotating head. Imperious and
haughty. It's not surprising the mysterious
Owl has meddled with people minds. Through
myth and folklore, we've managed to lay some
peculiar extra baggage on these 'all-seeing,
all-knowing' creatures over the years. Holding
vigils for virgins? Harbingers of horror?
Wizard's wingmen? Or simply a marvellous
niche invention for the afterhours?

Whatever they are up to, they are a personal
favourite of mine and my band British Sea
Power. Perched amongst tree branches,
we often employ decoy 'Long-Eared Owls'
on stage. They watch over us, staring out into
the audience, giving us some added primeval
stage presence. The Owls are watching
yoooouuu-ooooo.

Martin Noble, August 2014

INTRODUCTION

It's simple: everybody loves owls! They are all things for all men – including all women and children. Tough, wise, spooky, scary, majestic, austere, spiritual, easy to draw, inspirational and cute.

In a work of wonder, every family of owl has evolved totemic skills for survival in habitats around the globe – from the lush woodlands of home, mountainside glades of the Himalayas and the world's peaks, savannahs of Africa, dust-bowls of the Americas and the equatorial tropical rainforest everywhere south of the meridian.

However we like to depict the owl, their unique individuality throughout the species and their unflinching colonisation of our Earth is simply breathtaking.

And that is why I love owls.

WOODLAND
OWLS

Barn Owl
Tyto alba

Easily one of the most beautiful, elegant
and enigmatic of all animals, never mind owls,
the Barn Owl is transcendental to view in
the wild: a shining pure illumination and the
darkest of eyes unfathomably deep.

They were not always deemed this way, and so
the legend of owls as cursed creatures, ill-fated
doom-bringers of destruction arose from this
spectral bird, whose call is a bloodcurdling
shriek that could strip the fingernails from all
those unfortunate enough to meet it. A wing
or even a whole Barn Owl would be nailed to
a barn door to keep out all witchery ways and
evil doings, so feared and ominous were they.

But however they got their name, Barn
Owls are a natural wonder. They are found
all around the world on silent wingbeats,
with a face you could never forget.

Pygmy Owl
Glaucidium passerinum

This bushy-eyebrowed owl bumbles
around the woods hunting birds twice
his size, like a pocket-sized politician after
a liquid lunch, frequenting many a glade
stretching across northern America, central
Europe and many parts of Asia. There are a
few variants of this little fellow, notably the
Northern, Ferruginous, Andean and Cuban
Pygmy Owls, depending on where you're
looking. But whichever one you see, they
will all be roughly the height of a new pencil –
with much of that being their head.

Little Owl
Athene noctua

To us, the Little Owl is the small, dumpy one that sits on a fence post at dusk, watching the traffic fly by. But in days of yore, the mighty *Athene noctua* was an omnipotent symbol of wisdom, good fortune and sobriety. He was the bird of the Greek goddess Athene, upon whose shoulder he alighted, her sagacious terracotta companion – just like the ones illustrated on ancient red pots in museums and now too in the present day: iconised on charms and keepsakes from municipal markets and tourist traps across Greece.

The Acropolis was once full of Little Owls, living amongst the pillars and rocks, looking down upon a great civilisation. Today, they are found across the whole of Europe and Asia.

Tawny Owl
Strix aluco

Perhaps the wisest of all our owls – or the
wisest-looking anyway – and also a little bit
forgetful, slapdash, sleepy and maybe even
a little bit grumpy too. As we know with all
great brainiacs, their genius goes hand in
hand with just as much of a lack of patience,
self-hygiene and common sense. Not that
I'm saying that the tawny is scruffy; it's just
that he looks like he fell asleep and fell out
of his tree into a big pile of leaves, and
bumbled back on with his day without
smartening himself back up again.

Being honest, owls aren't the brightest
of birds, amazing as they are; parrots and
crows are much smarter. It's all in the eyes:
those magnificent piercing optics are what
make all owls look like they are deep in
concentrated scrutiny and wallowing
in long-lost knowledge.

Striped Owl
Pseudoscops clamator

The Striped Owl is the Long-Eared Owl's
chilled-out cousin from South America ...
Or is he? Scientists have struggled with stripy
genius's genus – so he has been awarded his
own family name of *Pseudoscops*, along with
a small handful of other rogue avian rarities.
That's how he earned his stripes.

Aside from the sound-channelling facial
disc, most owls have an amazing structural
display of feathers across their chest – an
arrangement as accomplished as Persian
architecture; a perfect chaos governed by
the mathematics of the universe.

Long-Eared Owl
Asio otus

A tall, elegant bird who would rather eat you than do herself the disservice of actually looking at you. With a scowl that could send an icy shiver down the binoculars of whomever dared to gaze upon her – before petrifying the stoutest of hearts. Rendering you stricken like a plastic bird scarer and eternally statued, with internal nightmares of past fashion choices …

'Did I really wear that anorak?' Moody.

Short-Eared Owl
Asio flammeus

Caught in the sunny daytime after she has been
up all night, with a face like thunder, mid-walk
of shame, flying over open ground looking for
her purse, mascara smeared with a behemoth
of a hangover. Don't get in her way, don't talk
to her, just let her do what she's doing and let
her get back to bed. She needs her kip.

Jamaican Owl
Pseudoscops grammicus

As the name suggests, this rufous warm owl is only found on that beautiful island in the West Indies. Another anomaly for the scientists, what with their Eagle-Owl ears and the semblance of a stupendous 'scops' owl – and so we have another curious entrant to the exclusive *Pseudoscops* subdivision.

Sadly our friend is not a great traveller and not a fraction as successful as many of Jamaica's other exports that have circumnavigated the globe. If only they were as popular as reggae, they wouldn't be on the endangered list.

Collared Scops Owl
Otus bakkamoena

A witch's tapestry of dusty moth's wing,
flaked pages from an alchemist's compendium,
lichen and moss, intricately woven together
with spiders' webs and Swallow spit. Found
high in the trees of temperate forests across
much of Asia, it's easy to see why a bird
as bizarre and curious-looking as the
Collared Scops has been associated with
magical myths and properties from
all corners of the Far East.

Northern Saw-Whet Owl
Aegolius acadicus

OMG SO CUUUTTTEEE!!!
Yup, the Northern Saw-Whet Owl is an
absolute darling, with a permanent look
of surprise spread across its adorable little
face, its smaller-than-a-blackbird and
fluffier-than-a-three-week-old–Labrador,
and with pleading puppy dog eyes
that look at you like you're about to give
him the biggest chocolate mouse he has
ever seen. One of the smallest owls in
North America and just as popular with
bird lovers as it is with ALL CAP
shouters on YouTube.

TROPICAL
OWLS

Greater Sooty Owl
Tyto tenebricosa

A negative Barn Owl. A lot of Australian animals are a bit dark, from the bloodthirsty crocs to the highly toxic spiders and snakes; and they also have a massive emu relative called a Cassowary that can rear up and disembowel any foolsome backpacker getting in its way.

But this Goth Barn Owl is not dangerous in any way – except to the small rodents and bugs that he stalks through the eucalyptus forests of northern Australia, with his jet-black wizard's cloak contrasting brilliantly with his white markings, shining as bright as the stars of the southern hemisphere.

Oriental Bay Owl
Phodilus badius

If people in the olden days thought Barn Owls were spooky and cursed, just imagine what they would have made of an Oriental Bay Owl. A twisted vision, a nightmare stalking, a vilesome monstrosity!

Owls have been used symbolically in art for centuries; their looming presence, bloodcurdling calls and fearsome hunting techniques have represented nightmares and oft suggested a sense of foreboding and horror. So although this is practically a *Tyto* family member, I still can't help but picture it as the wretched soul of a beloved Barn Owl trapped in purgatory. And that is exactly why they still have a power over the human race – the owls are not what they seem …

Maned Owl
Jubula lettii

Deep in the rainforests of Western Africa,
a maned hunter basks in his kingdom, but
this one has tufts and tassels rather than a
thick imperial beard, and he probably has one
mate – if he's lucky – rather than a harem at
his padded paws. But still, he is an amazing-
looking owl, whomever you want
to compare him to.

Barred Eagle-Owl
Bubo sumatranus

An owl walks into a pub. The landlord says,
'I'm not serving you!'

The owl says, 'Why not?'

'Cos you're barred!'

Sorry.

'Dad gags' aside, the Barred Eagle-Owl is
a moderately large Wood Owl, and a beautiful
addition to any coniferous woodland across
the whole of North America and Mexico.
Even though he is quite common, he still
retains mystique, looking like a nomad of the
forest with exotic gypsy blood, shrouded in
a shemagh scarf, singing his questioning,
classic song of 'Who cooks for you?'

Certainly not the landlord!

Spectacled Owl
Pulsatrix perspicillata

Dwelling in the lush rainforests of
Central America, striking, handsome and
uncomplicated, these Spectacled Owls have
no need for camouflage or anything else like
that. Just a distinguishing pair of eyeglasses
to cut them a fly look in the jungle.

But watch out: their wide-eyed optimistic
beam can quickly switch to a malevolent glare.
Much as an exasperated teacher might fix you
with an icy stare above her bifocals. Chilling.

Long-Whiskered Owlet
Xenoglaux loweryi

Who have we got here, then? Despite an
appearance to the contrary, this is a fully
grown Pygmy Owl and not a baby career-
politician – a wild-eyebrowed, know-it-all
toddler perched on a leather chesterfield
giving his opinionated opinions to the
rest of the woods.

So don't let those overabundant whiskers and
his bookish demeanour put you off: the Long-
Whiskered Owlet is an amazing bird, found
solely in the cloud forests on the hills of the
Andes in Peru – a magical, impenetrable land
that has gone untouched for millennia and is
home to so many other natural wonders as yet
unknown to mankind. Let's just try
to leave them to it.

Black-and-White Owl
Strix nigrolineata

This pied owl is a desperado of the subtropical forests of Central America, a smart stippled bird donning a bandito mask to rob the hot, damp woodland of its cicadas.

Although they do see very well in the dark, all owls have very bad eyesight close up – and won't be able to tell if you're sticking your tongue out at them. Handy. Yet all possess a moustache of stiff whiskery feathers around the beak, which are an essential tool for hunting any time of the day.

Spotted Wood Owl
Strix seloputo

A gorgeous owl that brings a touch
of autumnal panache across the whole of
Southeast Asia. The orange-eyed owl is
crepuscular – hunting at dusk and dawn,
timing his body clock with those of his prey.
The yellow-irised owls are diurnal – daytime
hunters. The eyes are the gateway to
the ~~soul~~ stomach!

Buff-Fronted Owl
Aegolius harrisii

What a dull name for such a visually vibrant
owl. It's a shame the bods who named him
concentrated on the buff chest rather than
the massive 'V' emblazoned across his face.
How could you miss that?

With this chap, 'V' most definitely stands for
'verve'; and also for 'Venezuela', which is one
of the countries in Central America where you
will find him, as well as many other breeds
of our amazing tropical owls.

Fearful Owl
Nesasio solomonensis

What an awesome name for a beast of an
owl, with his razor-sharp claws, bulky frame
and vexed facial markings. That 'X' across
his countenance illuminates a terrifying beak
that strikes fear into any possum, phalanger,
parrot or poacher that treads through the
forests of the Fearful Owl.

Not much is known about the fellow, being
a rare breed living in inhospitable terrain. He
does look very similar to the bygone Laughing
Owl from New Zealand, who is sadly extinct.
With deforestation and decreasing food
sources in the Solomon Isles, this could very
easily be the fate of this rare owl too.

Maybe that's why he is so fearful.

Crested Owl
Lophostrix cristata

Another owl from the Neotropics and found all across Central and South America. Roughly the size of a Barn Owl – but those eyebrows must measure him up against an Eagle-Owl. What incredible appendages! They are very handy, and not just to fan our hero in the hot, humid jungle. In fact, they are used in a variety of ways. Straight up or tucked away when he's feeling threatened and pretending to be a branch; out at 45 degrees when he is alert; flopped out and hanging down sideways when he's just chillin', man.

Brown Fish Owl
Bubo zeylonensis

A large Eagle-Owl like this chap was probably once a barbarian meat-lover who found himself trapped in a spot with just seafood for dinner, took a liking to it, and then turned pescetarian. So, through time and evolution, he has done away with the facial disc of a sound-hunting owl to develop a sharper, eagle-like head. Who needs ears to catch a fish anyway; when was the last time you heard a trout?

The Brown Fish Owl was always believed to be a bird of Asia and the Middle East – until some keen-eyed twitcher discovered a pair in a beautiful lake idyll hidden away in Turkey. The owls took roost and have fledged into a nice colony of Baykuş – which translates to Mr Bird. Finally: a little bit of respect!

African Wood Owl
Strix woodfordii

He's from Africa and he lives in the woods.

A recognisable relative of our Tawny Owl,
whose coat echoes his surroundings just as
much as the tangerine-and-chestnut outfit of
the fine Tawny mirrors the lush copse that he
calls home. With the jungle's dense bronze-
and-auburn tones highlighted with white
spots – which look like stars reflected in the
still, sepia pools of the rainforest – the African
Wood Owl wears his heart on his sleeve.

WILDERNESS
OWLS

Ural Owl
Strix uralensis

Am I allowed to have a favourite? If I was,
it would certainly be the lovely Ural Owl.
They haunt the Ural mountain forests and
Siberian steppes like friendly ghosts with their
coats the colour of smoke flecked with ash,
their immense midnight eyes that you could
drown in, and a big tough beak that clacks like
coconut husks. Their presence is pleasant and
can seem somewhat dainty, but as with
all owls, appearances can be deceptive. The
Ural Owl is known as one of the hardest
owls going – and rules his patch as
mercilessly as a Mongol Khan.

Scops Owl
Otus scops

There are little Scops Owls pretending
to be branches and keeping tucked away in
every corner of the world where it is warm.
This common Scops is Europe's initiate
in what is probably the biggest chapter of
owl species. They are available in a range of
different shapes, sizes and colour tones but all
come with charming, tufty ears and an amazing
flecked pattern: a dazzling camouflage for
the dense woodland, tropical rainforest
and bamboo thickets in which they
hide and reside.

Flammulated Owl
Psiloscops flammeolus

I was a bit disappointed when I looked up
'flammulated' in the dictionary; it doesn't
mean 'flammable feathers', nor is it a fancy
phrase for a forest fire. It just means 'a reddish
colour', which, if you ask me, is a bit of a dull
moniker for one of the oddest and smallest
owls in America – especially when you factor
in a coat of feathers as incredible as his. He
looks like a little wet owl who has been rolled
in a dusty elixir – a potion concocted from
a pinch of leaves from an autumnal, amber
forest floor, which are then delicately crushed
to a fiery dust and transfused with a handful
of sparks, and a bit of eye of newt, toe of frog
mixed in for good measure. Magic!

Eurasian Eagle-Owl
Bubo bubo

Talons like butcher's hooks, wings like pub doors, a massive neck like a Turkish weightlifter, this owl has a swagger like he knows everybody in the room – and knows everybody is scared of him. Yet he's still approachable and actually very likeable.

It is highly likely that you have seen one – and if you have ever been to an owl centre, you may even have held one. Yes, the Eurasian Eagle-Owl was the enormous, elephantine owl who was happy to stand on your be-gloved, beloved hand but who, just as you were starting to feel comfortable, gave you a look as if to say: 'Oi, I'm in charge and I can easily snap that hand clean off.' Gulp!

Blakiston's Fish Owl
Bubo blakistoni

Whose style is less elegant fly fisherman and more like a poacher on a moonless night; who waits in the shadows, perched on bankside stumps, coarse trousers held up with a length of bailing twine, ferret in his back pocket and a brace of pheasants over his shoulder. There, on low-slung branches, he lingers, waiting to drop down into the icy waters to grope for unsuspecting fish in the chilling mountain streams of Japan and Russia.

Snowy Owl
Bubo scandiacus

A coat of the purest white and an icy stare
as piercing as a north-easterly wind. Females
and the young have coal-black spots and bars,
but all are magnificently milky: a perfect
camouflage, much better than that of polar
bears and arctic foxes, who of course are white,
but have a wee bit of a yellowy tint against
their bleached surroundings.

A monarch of the tundra, the Snowy Owl is a
whopper and close to an Eagle-Owl in height
and hunting prowess, feeding upon lemmings,
ptarmigans and other winter fare by snatching
her prey with her massive moonboots. Her
feet are ensconced in thick feathers to protect
against the cruel temperatures of the arctic and
styled in a brilliance of frosted white.

Hawk Owl
Surnia ulula

Here we have a precise and vicious
pursuant of voles and other small fluffy
rodents, chasing them through the cold,
pine-scented forests of the northern part
of America, Canada, Scandinavia,
Russia and China.

The Huntsman: he has the eyes of a hawk,
the long tail of a hawk, the low mean brow
of a hawk and the stripy T-shirt of a hawk –
whilst also possessing the bulky wings of
an owl, the specialised facial disk of an owl
and the feather-taloned boots of an owl.
So when you combine these special weapons
and tactics you can have nothing but the
unique … Hawk Owl!

Great Grey Owl
Strix nebulosa

Yes, he is great, isn't he? With a head like a
geodesic dome inhabited by a bunch of strung-
out hippies, the Great Grey Owl looks like
he's been hanging out with these guys for some
time. With a wide-eyed mellowness, he takes in
the world at his own pace.

But don't let that mellow vibe fool you: hidden
within that massive owl-down puffa jacket
is a stealthy hunter, whose body was built to
survive the glacial northern quarters of the
world in Asia, America and Europe. His tightly
knitted helmet works as an intricate feathered
vortex, channelling the sound of mice going
about their day under thick snow. The Great
Grey Owl tunes into the vibrations emanating
from the rodent's tunnelled networks …
before expertly dropping down to pick out his
prey. An energy-saving tactic to survive the
bitter conditions of his sub-zero domain.

Boreal Owl
Aegolius funereus

Another owl from the same dense hyperborean
forests as the Hawk Owl spread across the
world just before the trees meet the tundra.
An owl with many a moniker, it is known
more commonly here as the Tengmalm's Owl,
but it also answers to the Richardson's Owl
and Pearly Owl too. But I like 'Boreal', as it is
basically a posh way of saying 'cold forest'.

But whatever you want to call it, you can
always recognise it as the owl with the head the
shape of an upside-down skip, or to give it a
scientific twist – a Boreal Owl with a
crown like a wobbly trapezium.

Giant Scops Owl
Otus gurneyi

In the kingdom of the minuscule Scops,
you don't have to be much bigger than a
pigeon to be regarded as colossal amongst
your equals. This tiny giant strides across his
teeny kingdom – made up of only three small
mountainous islands in the Philippines – with
a pelt as winningly optimistic and sanguine as
an equinoxical sun. Positive is what he needs to
be, as deforestation and mining are flattening
his home and destroying his habitat.

Jungle Owlet
Glaucidium radiatum

This owl could easily sit on your shelf:
a polished teak talisman; a memento of your
travels to distant misty lands. Not much bigger
than a bullfinch, this toy-sized Pygmy Owl
has a beautiful plot that he can call home. His
stomping ground is the moist deciduous forest
that stretches all the way across the foothills
of the Himalayas. What a view!

He may be small, but he certainly knows how
to pick the best neck of the woods.

DESERT
OWLS

White-Faced Scops Owl
Ptilopsis leucotis

With the waxy whiskers of a Mandarin
kung-fu wizard, the Northern White-Faced
Owl from the savannahs of Africa is
a magnificent magician of mutation.

At ease, the White-Faced Owl is quite
handsome and striking, with his monochrome
face, orange eyes and silver-fox moustache.
Under threat from a similar sized villain,
he fans his wings and bobs his head with
fantastical fiery eyes – an awesome defensive
tactic used by many owls. But whilst in the
presence of a large predator, he draws in all
his feathers, turns sideways and makes himself
as slim as possible. With squinting eyes and a
beak completely covered in an oily bush, the
owl now resembles a braided, bonkers branch.
So, really not handsome in the slightest.

Great Horned Owl
Bubo virginianus

From his leafy temple in the North
Country to the desert wastelands of the
Deep South, the Worshipful Master of
the Americas governs the land with iron
talons. An aggressive predator who demands
respect, he appears like the ancient god
Moloch, presiding over sombre sacrificial
rites in the torch-lit caves of his ancestors.
Easily the largest owl of the land,
and effortlessly the most dangerous:
the all-seeing head of the totem.

Southern Boobook Owl
Ninox novaeseelandiae

Bubuk is the Aboriginal name for this
small Hawk Owl; it's a term used widely
across Australia to describe a variety of owls.
Its other names include Ngugug, Morepork
and Mopoke, which are all onomatopoeias
describing the gruff croak of Australia's
smallest and most common owl.

All owls have fourteen vertebrae in
their long necks – that's twice as many as
us humans – and they can turn their heads
almost completely upside down. Strewth!

Spotted Eagle-Owl
Bubo africanus

Yes, it's got ear tufts, making it an
Eagle-Owl, and spots, making it a Spotted
Eagle-Owl. But that's all rather prosaic-
sounding for a wonderfully illuminated bird
like this, which looks as though it's made out
of delicate, crisp layers of Viennetta ice cream
and 90 per cent dark chocolate drops.

At 45cm, this gent is one of the smaller owls,
but quite a common and most welcome spot
with the binoculars if you are out jotting in the
hot, arid woodland of northern Africa or
the Arabian Peninsula.

As a bird with ice-cream feathers, only
one label will suffice. Cool owl!

Verreaux's Eagle-Owl
Bubo lacteus

All right, cheeky! Who are you batting
those lashes at?

As owls go, the Verreaux is up there with
the biggest and heaviest – but that only means
he weighs the same as a hedgehog. It's those
hollow bones and the hunter-gatherer diet
that keeps him trim.

This African Eagle-Owl of the Sahara is
a perfect example of how owls' specialist
eyesight works. Those heavy lids are to protect
the binocular-like, independently moving,
tubular eyes that sit still and stationary inside
the sockets – unlike our eyeballs, which can
roll around. To compensate for the lack of
movement, they bob their heads to and fro
and twist their necks round 270 degrees.
That's not all the way round; if they tried
that, their heads would pop off!

Pel's Fishing Owl
Scotopelia peli

The African Fishing Owls are a different kettle of fish to the Asian Fishing Owls. They are much more proud of their appearance and don't have the funny shrunken-head thing going on.

Pel's is quite the opposite to that, in fact, and is able to display his fine head of feathers into a glorious rufous full crown when the moment takes him. It must be one of the finest sights in nature to see a Pel's Fishing Owl in its natural surroundings. What a spot!

Elf Owl
Micrathene whitneyi

As you can imagine, the Elf Owl is one of
our smallest owls. A member of the Pygmy
family, who inhabits the famous Wild West
deserts of the USA and Mexico.

I think it would be fair to say that the
Elf Owl loves cacti, especially the saguaro; the
famous type that stands sentinel and looks like
a silhouette of a swollen, surrendering cowboy
(without a hat) against the red desert sky.

It's no wonder they love them – as the cacti
are an ecosystem that provides everything our
friend needs. Food: the insects visiting the
cactus's flowers and fruit. Shade: against the
searing desolate sun. Shelter: our owl nests in
holes carved out by sap-loving woodpeckers.
What's not to love?

Powerful Owl
Ninox strenua

I doff my cap to the pioneer in deepest
Australia who first clapped eyes on this
strapping beast – probably while it was
ripping off a koala's head – and baptised
it the Powerful Owl.

Bounding in at 65cm high, it's a member
of the hawk family; so it has a strange, round
head like a hairy buzzard, with a cleaver-like
beak and feet like sharpened anchors.

As you can tell from its great name, Powerful
is the largest and most feared Australian owl.

Burrowing Owl
Athene cunicularia

This stern little troglodyte is a member
of the Little Owl family who has found
himself with a unique roosting style amongst
his peers. A bird of the Americas, living
wherever there are dry ranges and open
grassland – or, to be precise, the panoramas
where you will find prairie dogs and their
burrows – as that is where the Burrowing
Owl likes to bury his head.

You can't see them in this illustration as she
is obviously burrowing, but this owl actually
has quite long legs and is a remarkable sprinter
– making her just as agile on the foot as on
the wing, and a hunter with auspicious talents.
She even inspired the Native Americans to
herald the Burrowing Owl as a protective
spirit for their warriors.

Stygian Owl
Asio stygius

An even moodier Moody Long-Eared Owl,
how can this be? I had heard talk of such a
phantom, and my eyes do not deceive me! The
Stygian Owl is a shadowy, horned apparition
that haunts Central and South America, with a
death-like glare – and a name to match.

'Stygian' is derived from the River Styx,
the waterway from the Greek myths. There
is a saying of being 'as dark as the River Styx'
and it was a murky place indeed: a grim course
of black water, where the Reaper-like boatman
Charon ferried the souls of the dead to the
underworld kingdom of Hades. It seems
like the ancient Greeks thought the same
way about Long-Eared Owls as I do, but to
be honest, I am more concerned about the
demonic, capitalist Great Horned Owl
than the grumpy Stygian and his
cantankerous *Asio* brothers.

Brown Wood Owl
Strix leptogrammica

An owl made of mahogany, with a facial-disc
fade of titian red to fresh ginger – so not just
'brown', and therefore much deserving of a
better name. Even the mouthful of his Latin
name of leptogrammica just means 'finely
barred', which she most certainly is. However,
on inspection, the trunk coat of all large owls
is an outstanding lattice of layered softness,
with the feathers having a velvet comb of
serrated tips that cushion sound and aid the
silent flight of these hushed hunters.

Dusky Eagle-Owl
Bubo coromandus

A ravishing khaki owl of India and
Southeast Asia. The life of a Dusky sounds
like nirvana – his bungalow is built in the
cool, leafy heights of old mango or tamarind
trees, with its veranda facing the riverside.
Here, escaping the hullabaloo, he and his good
wife reside all year round and take tiffin at
dusk, consisting of the local avifauna.
Sounds pukka.

Omani Owl
Strix omanensis

Last but by no means least, here we have
an owl who was very late to the party – so late,
in fact, that if I had created this book just a
year earlier, this fine bird would not have
even been discovered yet.

The rocky, scattered hillside groves of Omani
in the Middle East are where two expert
bird-sound recordists chanced upon this rare
Arabian treasure. Very much a Desert Owl in
colouring – but with long legs, orange eyes
and a distinct call to set it apart from the
local, but also unique, Hulme's Tawny Owl of
the same locality. All of these characteristics
told the recordists straight away that they
had discovered a new species to add to our
wonderful world of owls. Let's raise a drink
to the guys with the sound approach.

SPOTTING AND JOTTING

It's great spotting an owl you've never seen before, so here's a handy way of keeping all your jottings in check. Get spotting either by sitting comfortably at your window, or pack your boots, a flask and binoculars, and go on your travels across the globe. Happy spotting!

☑ Barn Owl

☑ Pygmy Owl

 ☑ Little Owl

 ☑ Tawny Owl

 ☑ Striped Owl

☑ Long-Eared Owl

☑ Short-Eared Owl

☑ Jamaican Owl

☑ Collared Scops Owl

 ☑ Northern
Saw-Whet Owl

 ☑ Greater
Scooty Owl

 ☑ Oriental
Bay Owl

 ☑ Maned Owl

 ☑ Barred Eagle-Owl

 ☑ Spectacled Owl

 ☑ Long-Whiskered Owlet

☑ Black-and-White Owl

☑ Spotted
Wood Owl

☑ Buff-Fronted Owl

Fearful Owl

Crested Owl

Brown Fish Owl

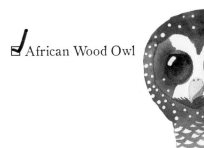
☑ African Wood Owl

☑ Ural Owl

☑ Scops Owl

☑ Flammulated Owl

☐ Eurasion Eagle-Owl

☑ Blakiston's Fish Owl

☑ Snowy Owl

☑ Hawk Owl

☑ Great
Grey Owl

☑ Boreal Owl

☑ Giant Scops Owl

☑ Jungle Owlet

☑ White-Faced Scops Owl

☑ Great Horned Owl

☑ Southern
Boobook Owl

☑ Spotted
Eagle-Owl

☑ Verraux's
Eagle-Owl

Pel's Fishing Owl

Elf Owl

Powerful Owl

Burrowing Owl

☑Stygian Owl

☑Brown Wood Owl

☑Dusky Eagle-Owl

☑Omani Owl

ACKNOWLEDGEMENTS

Thank you to:

The Goldfinches, The Sewells, The Roses
and the Lees.

Martin Noble, Simon Benham, Nicki, Jeff,
Robin and Andrew at Caught By The River.

Fizz, Jambo, Milley, Pip, Boo, Paul and
Mark at Battlefield Falconry Centre.

Phil Aylen, Edward Lear, Eleazar Albin,
Boran Biriz, Roy Wilkinson, Ceri Levi
and the internet.

Find out more about Matt and his work at
www.mattsewell.co.uk